TORSINO

DARRELL KINSEY

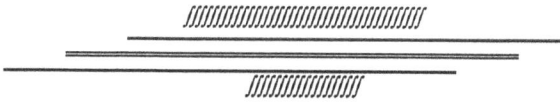

TORSINO

A BEVELED MIRROR BOOK
Published by Kinsey Publishing
131 East Broad Street
Number 205
Athens, Georgia 30601

ISBN 978-0-6151-9074-7

To Loudelle

Part I

Everything that is was once something else. The casual smoke rise was once liquid in the pan, and I was he back then. You were she before torsino made it something else. The magic is in the transition, and the wind up is in slow motion, like trying to talk in the middle of a yawn. Get up at dawn to see that the morning was once something else, and the sky was divided and undecided today, having been all the colors found in both fruit and bruises. And so have I, and so have you too.

Black Blanket

We live like the French used to.
Remember the party in the four-man tent
when the morning was just starting to tug
at the corners of the black blanket on the world?
Strange lightning bugs came flirting with each other,
their inclinations ostensible even through the canvas ceiling.
Your bathing suit was revealing,
and the beaujolais in your belly button
was hard to drink without slurping; so rude.

Waking Up Naturally

In smoking wine,
the fumes blue the palette
like a bruise on the ceiling,
and the hood lamp shows the most
varicose steam, rising in ropes
through a sheer windpipe.
The beginning of springtime in the south,
upstairs in the hall,
tubes of fluorescent lighting,
dying in the ceiling,
send flickers to the pinwheel
spinning taped to the window sill.
The zone of dawn hangs by
as a thrilling threat to the burned wine.
They're sexy together,
and they curl like calling finger signals,
rolling simple in the condo,
straightforward and letting each other know
their notions of right away.
The smell of cum plants lifts us up,
so if we don't pay attention,
we wake up laughing.

Face of the Deep

March is underwater
when light creeps to the fringe times,
the floor and ceiling of the day.
Thinking is like dreaming
with the feeling of humpback whales
and sounds that are played through broken speakers.
The beginning of springtime in the south,
God has gone outside again,
and all cold is quicker now.

Her Description of an Album

The silkscreen horse
and black ink has gotten
into the cotton.
Multitudes stagger.
Riding with scoliosis
and whipping myself faster
toward where gypsies enter heaven.
It makes me feel important.

Part II

Have a spark with a bull, and its breath in my hands, wet while we pet for a second. Then its horn feels good in me, and I am lifted up, eyes closed against the sun, warm, and the bluest part of the sky forms with my bloody hand in front of it, a cinematic fade-in of purple oil, the color of bull love, and I wear the stains to work because I like the way they smell, osmophilius as hell. My lunch breaks are almost always like this.

Rain in the Shower

The power is out.
Getting clean by flashlight
from the showerhead in the wall to your body.
Broken streams in the beam
are excited white like tracer bullets,
and the dropped dollop of conditioner
streaks the lens with residue,
so the display of light
is a white slice of tomato against the bathrobe plaid.
The power comes back
while you drip solution on your contact,
but the electrical storm still dies in the hall.

Plaid Shirt

Your background is pure,
and I see a stripe of insight,
in you a line of kind,
hemmed genuine.
Embroidered aorta,
bright brown,
and when you're blue you apologize,
little orange flirt.
You have on a bad ass plaid shirt.
I want more to do with your collarbone.

Parked by the Curb

Don't know if it's barking.
The windows are up,
and the stereo face is orange and blue
and showing equalizer bars.
It looks like it is
in the chain-linked fence
rattling by the house.
The dog is brushing up against
the scabs of peeling paint.
He has padded and run the mud to black.
I wish I could wish on the porch
all day for the mailman.
Imagine him coming like a figure,
his color needing adjustment
and his vertical hold unstable.
This officer is walking
and dropping paper with glued plastic windows
in the red glitter of grit isles.
Delivery songs sound like whistles
that come from back there in those trees.

Bambi Is Young

Holding the branch back
from the side mirror
so you can check the rain
sitting in balls on your head.
This kind makes your hair white.
Smash it slick,
and skirt fat leaf drops.
It's too early for shorts,
but we both have them on,
stepping over the guardrail
and walking in tall grass by the road.

A Good Lunch Break

Go ahead and do the rap
about the flowers
in the little plot of bed
outside the office building.
Rhyme about pink.
I can read the newspaper ink
growing in on the trunks of trees.
It says little films on little screens,
Little Kings in a little while.
The fastest trees grow claymation-style,
and the color of cover art is fuzzy on the twigs,
the texture of packaging material,
and the limbs form like your pelvic bones.
Remembering them on medical film,
still turns me on,
blue and gray XXX-ray.
Rap with the high hat.
Rap about the office buildings
in a lowland bend of the bypass.

Pinot Grigio

I'm afraid to take out
my pinot grigio.
The tiny arm brushed by it
and felt its temperature,
and some of the movie
showed on the grass bank
like a talking chin in a scene,
and she may not even want my pinot grigio.
Some say they don't want it with verisimilitude.
My pinot grigio isn't nude.
It's in my knapsack next to my lawn chair,
and I brought a tool for the cork.
Cold white sloshing in the bottle.
I looked behind me at the house,
rising high and narrow in the field.
I want to take out my pinot grigio,
but I think they might see it
in the movie light,
banded across the sky
like yarn in a loom.

Thursday Nights

I'm in heaven. It's like a hallucination on earth.

It's like before my birth, I hung out here,
déjà vu in front of a mirror.

And my beard is like God's. I sit on his thigh.

It's weird, weird
to look down at the sky.

Feelings about Gym Shorts

In yellow gym shorts,
watching TV,
Chloe Sevigny.

The show is sad
and your eyes.

Rest Friends

God doesn't lie
except on Sunday,
like a monolith on a love seat
on your sabbath
when nothing is done.

We don't lie
except on Sundays
with my ear above your heart
and my heart above your part that glows,
and the rest of the time,
he is standing up working,
sending rabbits to run across our graves.

I work in an office,
and you work in a café.

Great of You to Notice

The living room is the dead room,
and the bedroom is the place to be.
Come look at the wall art tonight,
blue and orange rectangles
made by the streetlights.
They're different every bedtime.
We're tired.
The sheets are cool,
and the comforter is heavy.

Muscles Love Bones

The segue of a leg
into a torso,
more so than others,
that's what I love.

The segue of an arm
into a breast farm,
does me no harm
to kiss it there.

Her legs have muscles,
and muscles love bones.

They hug them to move.

Part III

They looked at the map. The Gulf of Mexico was round and curving, labeled in blue italics. "I've been down there a hundred times, but I can't imagine what's happening there right now, like right now," he said.

"That's why people travel," her message behind her curves in hot pink italics.

Museum Boat

The museum boat picked us up
at Cape San Blas
and rolled out through thin water,
the sun like wire filaments
in the bulb of gulf
that the purple flying fish
broke before the bow.
In the cabin, ornate frames
with brass show lamps
cramped the edges of the Mona Lisa,
so much so, you could barely understand the painting.
Mating is as common as a dish towel
and as ceremonious as a handkerchief, I explained,
and you quietly asked to be taken to the snack counter.

Dark and Down

Cool block wall painted Cuba blue,
you lean against it in black tennis shoes
and base on litmus bathing suit
listening to the voice box of a man
through a sleek little boom box half-buried in the sand.
You got it so loud, his fingers on the strings
remind me of you zipping up the front
of that neon windbreaker you wore when you were down.
Down in the park,
the disengaged forklift holds a palm tree.
Breeze-fondled fronds and roots bundled tight,
I'd like to unhook the bungees on its burlap wrap
and nuzzle my face in your full dark triangle.

Cleome

Such sad scissors I used.
They were blue
plastic on the handle,
and the falling on air
to the bathmat.
I'll miss the spiders
between your pink elastic
and your wet leg.
Covered in part of the pool,
some you brought out on you
and some you dripped back
from the top step by the rail.

Pastelia

Panama Jack looks lonely
on that boy's back.
The colors I loved as a youth,
the colors of a swimsuit.
When he took off his white blazer,
we saw that he had been sweating.
He loved her,
and we were glad they got to be together
in a bed for a change.
The air conditioner actually made it feel cool.
Pastel walls.
Pastelia actually is the world he lives in,
and he has named it that forever.

Dark Compared to Outside

Hotels spread out
along the beach.
Hotels fat in the meridian sap.
I'd like to go into one
and be in one's lobby.
Automatic glass slides
and air conditioning smells like jungle.
Coconut products in hotels.
Plush fabric between wicker
and a flicker through fronds.
Hotels I own.
Hotels I slap.
Hotels with paths through gravel.
Landscaping is shaping a bush
with leathery leaves.
Hotels I love
and want to rub,
but I've never blown a bulb
in one of their rooms.

Meridian Break

Condominium a way of life
that leaves me dripping
chlorine from the lagoon of pool
all over the elevator gold.
Watch me riding through the floor bells,
my drawstring in the mirror
under my stomach hair.
I swam under the waterfall
and swam in-sync with my father-in-law.
We lifted our legs,
and now I'm in the air-conditioned condo,
cold and big
with my skin drawing up under the half-globes.
I looked out over the gulf from the ninth floor,
all the windows a warm curving wall.

Penthouse Tracks

He pretends to know nothing modern,
so it's funny when she sees him
advance the track.
He knows to do that.
He keeps his hair at a length
like he's always trying to grow it out.
It will never touch the glass tabletop
when he bows to meet his full spoon of cereal,
and his apple slices are golden
and covered with milk on the carpet.

The track star over there
on the love seat,
you know he can move
and really get busy,
so it's funny when she sees him
doing nothing on the love seat.

These two are perverse in a weird way.
They're really up here in the same penthouse together.

Socializing

Told her I thought
her child's name was beautiful.
I lied,
and the child knew it,
solid sitting up in its crib
like a marble of pink statue
sunken in the deep end of a pool.

A Friend in Statham

Ate a dozen oysters
with my folding phone
by the tray and lemons.
Got them confused
and answered a shell,
Hey Odom.
He said a pearl
that I wrapped in cracker plastic.

Don't You Wish You Had Come to Lunch with Us?

She had the bandanna over her face
in the parking lot.
She was thug.
I had on a white polo
and a diamond ring on my hand,
so I was cool kid.
The sky was dappled lipizzaner
with storms rolling in,
one of those quick beach rains
that you can see coming in for thirty minutes.
Don't you wish you had come to lunch with us?

Blew by to the South

Oh boy your body hair is blowing.
The shark clouds ease behind the pines,
and a gang of needles dive into the deep end
and float over to us on the top step.
Stab them into my chlorine stiff hair
and wonder about safety.

Casual Performance

Chlorine my favorite thing,
smelled it lying next to me
with face on the chaise bands.
You remembered your towel.
How will you remember me?

Black and turquoise bathing suit,
drawstring out a coil all convolute.
This is magic I can cross off my list.

Thick Liquid Full of Salt

No one could not like it,
the taste of the Gulf of Mexico
and the smell.
You can tell it's down there
from up here by Ebro.
I can smell it on my fingers,
and my lips have it dried.
I'm not going to wash up at the rest stop.
I'm not going to wash up
until we go down again
to the Gulf of Mexico,
maybe two weekends from now
when Kim and Adam's condo is free.

Part IV

A bull sucking on a butterscotch snuck into the living room to watch kickboxing on the flat screen. One fighter got knocked down, and scared by the surround sound, the bull started to choke. Bright quote marks came from its ears, and tears soaked the fur under its eyes. Something happens. The candy dissolves. The bull is calm. The bull is alright, and cutting to commercial means a swell of music, which is such traditional insight.

Dream Soldier

The dream introduced itself
as an old war hero,
and it sat down beside me.
It all started over rights
to a raspberry field
in the light a
pink cloud makes.
Who gets to pick and lick
this one here?
The dream had a temper
and got animated to tell it.
Wearing velvet in the summer
would irritate anyone.
My family waited hungry for me
while I fought.

19 Torsino 7

The year of my friends
shaking on the beach.
They thought they were dancing,
but the island bottom buckled,
and they didn't have songs anymore.
The guitar smashed on the floor
in little splinters for their gritty feet to take in,
and flames in cracks of the concrete shot
taller than the buildings painted pink.
The afternoon sun didn't think highly
of being rivaled from the guts of us.
The pale blue twinkle in the mess of heaven
was used to baking laziness all day,
and old life that has been that way for seasons
vibrated then like a cell phone on a desk
or a ripe cocoon rattling.
Might open up with sizzling streamers soon.
But Benedict Mary had them take their
horns from their cases
and play jangle songs
to the faces propped on hands,
to the bodies curled fetally
in woe-is-me sand.
Looking around the square,
where underneath the fountain,
a mountain has just come up.
Speak now in parables would do you good.
Life is not a heartbreaking presence,
so don't get dejected.
Even on your deathbed,
you're courting her to pieces,
and you can't chase a butterfly,

but be still,
and see if one doesn't land on your blouse
to flirt with your red sash.
Her tight black curls were a backdrop
for her smooth speaking face.
Then their doing was her speech
because it was then in their ears,
but they made the doing their own,
dancing again in broken down Jamaica.

Concert in the Square

I want a summer star
in a blue T-shirt
looking down at a keyboard
with stored songs in a cooler for the trip.
The locals have come out of the shade
to dance in the square.
Benny flare
and pocket Julie,
sun-mouthed citizens,
with homes and pocketbooks
rolling by the sea.

Talk Shake

I went deaf in the earthquake,
the great torsino shaker,
when a loud noise was generated
from the tearing up of land.
Parked back
against the trunk of a palm,
I looked up into its
firework of fronds.
They slipped me a note
about the efforts,
the shortwave correspondence
and its coming to term.
I haven't heard, I said,
and the vibrations of speech
in my dusty sinuses were all.

Party Like a Rock

Party like a rock.
Party like a CVS.
I'm lost in my collar,
flipped up above my temples
and sunken neck.
Chin on my breastplate.
Above the ship run aground,
the fireworks sizzle loud
like when stereo wires
are about to fizzle out.
My cousin moves my hair
and pulls down my collar,
tries to whisper in my ear.
They're shooting them
from the back deck,
and that's stretched out to our reef.
Remember the grottoes I know.
Maybe the life down there
looks up at the burning cracks
and thinks of me,
how they display like my dreads.

Melon Talk

Got to the fruit stand
performed a handstand
heard the coins hit on the sidewalk
heard some melon talk
about my head.

Grammy Smith

My Grammy lives in Miami.
She wrote to me in a note
about a waitress
whose cheeks showed
and whose feathered tiara glowed
with the power a battery provides.
Grammy hides in South Beach
among the shirtless and bemused.
In her day, she was a floozy too.
I got the evidence
wrapped up in paisley tissue.
I'm wrapped up in the past,
thinking about Grammy cutting loose.
She was off the chain, I surmise,
and her flavor was rambunctious.
Unwrap the paisley to know it again.

Coconut

The bellhop swam to shore,
his hat seen between the white caps
like a jewel case to be protected.
Once on shore, he
immediately fell in love
with a beached coconut.
He tried to pick it up
with several sleazy lines.

Shed Printout

Went back in the shed.
Plugged in the antique copier
just to see would it work.
It did, and we had copies of our faces
before too long.
My hair's getting long.
It spread out on the glass plate.
That's not mirror reliable though.
Like the shadow on the sidewalk
I check myself by sometimes.
The display didn't make any sense though.

Pool Scared

We had to scoot over
on the top step of the pool.
Natalie, the four-year-old, wanted to squeeze in.
She got a spot beside the bellhop.
She looked up at him and started crying.
The bellhop had grown a beard.

Instinct of the Week

My baby, my baby,
my baby's missing,
and somebody just kicked me
in the back of my stomach.
Hey it was my baby.
I guess she just hasn't been born.

Natalie in Ringlet Almost

Natalie in ringlet almost
called the doctor herself,
her curls smashed by the receiver.
Footsteps on the stairs
and an ankle.

Natalie is stocky in romper boots
and her mother's northern shawl.
To be cold with fever in the tropics.
She strolls with fingers in her mouth
and talks softly to herself,
but the window pane is so close,
the glass hears her too.

The Bellhop and the Waiter

The bellhop and the waiter
walked to find a phone.
They walked past a concert
and a barking dog.
The car burned from the engine,
but the stereo still worked.

The bellhop was a little deaf from riding motorcycles as a boy.
He toyed with the muffler.

The waiter was deaf from when—
(he made a circle with his arms)
They're big. They're called sub-woofers.

Laughing at the Fan

Laughing at the fan.
It oscillates answers
to questions about my future.
No, it turns.

Laughing at my fam.
My brother
plays with the hi lo dials.
His styles are sub-tropical,
and that's why we need the fan.
We all live here together.

Bell Drop

Yes um hmm
Yes of course
His ribboned trousers
were wet
and caked with
vanilla sand.
He kept offering me mai tais
even though he had fallen
off the ship.

And he was the bellhop,
not the waiter.

Dresser

My girlfriend divorced me
or I got in trouble
for stealing grapes
from a customer
at a work permanent,
an homage to other lands
and tropical bearing fruit.
My reflection in that long mirror
with all the junk in front of it,
the nozzle of my youth
sprays sticky with how I live,
and what I want for certain
won't look good in daylight
or fit through the door really.

Met a Dream

Dreamed a dreamcatcher was full.
It held psychedelic relics,
too many of them,
and the colors exploded
into the white wall background.
Simple feather hanging there.
Saw the dream I had way back.
Sleeping with lace over my eyes,
the air glows roiled
in the steady dark bedroom,
drop tile-wards like
time-lapsed tops of cloud shots
and now hanging in the catcher
still pumping and cooking,
the tint sacks shake to filter.
See things I think when I sleep.
Balloons filled with paint pop,
and the pigments steam art sauce.
My brown legs in the sheets get covered.
I wrote on the sheets my dreams,
and they were in the language
I think in when I sleep.
I wake up and dump the dreamcatcher.
Its net is stretched but clean,
and I should really empty it more often.

Aqua Bangle

Your aqua bangle
slid down to your wrist
when you touched my sleeping cheek.

Part V

Muscles of torsino, parked above me breathing. Curved limbs of ribs fortify a heart I would have to cradle with both arms to hold. It's a big heart. It spreads your silk around. I found some lining my new birthday blazer. You charged it instead of paying cash, but it didn't make me mad.

Public Hair

The greatest love poems in the world
are in booklets with cardboard covers
and cover art of glitter hearts,
and they're sold in open air markets
from long folding tables
holding radials of prism light
in the haunted surfaces of bootleg CDs.
Braided nylon key chains lay for sale
next to the booklet of poems,
in which birds are frozen in flight
with unaroused Vs for wings,
and in the description of you,
"Some hair is pinned against your belly skin
by a little band of lace,"
your public hair is for everyone,
and it lives beyond the page.

Belongings

I want to kiss all your belongings,
the blue piece of pottery
cool to my summer mouth.
My finger in the handle ring
let's me dangle it by my side
while I pace on a phone call.

All the belongings that belong to you,
including your made up song
that hangs above the chaise lounge.
It feels like some tinsel to hold.

The pottery was made when I wasn't old,
and you were made when I was the same age.

I want to kiss all of my belongings
when you aren't at home.

Precious love I own
like everything I have,
the birdbath back there.

No different than a birdcage.

Blue Tube

Got a video to upload
of a sparrow bird
fluttering in place,
thinking of landing
on the curved blue tube
of a neon sign.
Thinking not,
it dove for the phone booth.
I got it all with my new camera phone,
a present buried in the pink grass
of my Easter basket.

The Great Kashimax

Hey hey
Bet you're still
filling my socks with ribbons.
Hey hey
We'll see at the precipice lunch.
The community below speaks in blows,
knuckles the meat beneath
the tweeting dragon ink.
To go down there and know
your peppered underarms.
Hey hey
I'll ride over, leaning forward
on the ram handles of my burgundy street bike,
and I'll bet you still put on me
that black-green robe of gold
that holds my curls on padded shoulders.
Hey hey
Take pictures of me,
my street clothes on the floor.
I'm the best at resting indecent.
Woe betide my cap on backwards.

A Run-In

The cold chills came in
sluggish after lunch.
I surprised her in her office
and saw a difference in her skin,
bunched and drawn in the purple light
that flickered down from the ceiling case.

Something has caused in her a feeling
at the bases of her blond arm hairs,
stiff beside her braided bracelet
and stiff beside her black and floral dress sleeves.

Another background to talk about,
musicians letting something fall
and crash between the wall and banister.
Shoddy download.
She said excuse me.

Airbrush Fight

I watch you dress
in the brown dress
that your arms come out of,
that your legs come out of,
and your breast plate,
I watch it shield the heart I love,
and your neck,
I watch it hold the head I hug,
and your face,
I watch it carry the eyes I kiss.

Then you pull out your makeup bag,
and we fight again
like we did in front of the airbrush man at the beach,
whose colors were insincere.

Paginate

Rouge spread out to the temples
by the eyes all lined.
Determined to be a danger
and a beauty made of iron.
Growing wads of light
so purple you can handle
and fixing everything for me
in the condo before the show.

The metal around the bulbs
heats up like a body.
We have places to be,
and I'm rolling,
undressed, messing up the sheets,
spread out like a land,
flat and warm.
In the sun in the window,
I'll be wearing lids for eyes
and getting up in sections
or as wholes or as whales.
Moaning in the front row
with the lights on my legs.

The Song Everyone Can Play

He is throwing down
the solid black body
into a bed of wires.
At all times in the basement,
I'm loving a secret with redness
inside my bright chest
and protecting a secret with blackness
inside my dark pants.

Old Wax Master

The skinny thug looked like
Abraham Lincoln
in a cheap suit,
a gray fabric like plastic
and hot splotched tie.
You introduced him as your ex,
and an orange-trimmed banner was above his head for me then.
It said, EVEN OLD WAX MASTER

Disrespect

I like Elvis's music,
but I don't like the King's.
He sits on his thrown
and doesn't move around the stage,
but the King doesn't know an instrument.
He just wears beautiful suits,
and one stoned was a winksome
in the stage lights
like the glint in the eye
of an animated whitetail deer
who wandered into the courtyard.
It was someone's mere figment
caused by indignant regard
of his own mercurial guitar work,
and what an example on that red poster there.

Your band practices on Thursday night?
Mine doesn't practice at all
because I'm not in a band,
and I like Elvis's music
better than yours.

Looking for Shopping

Experimental music swells
while we stare at the bookshelves,
packed in with the other customers.
I think and grip my face.
This music makes it seem
like something is about to happen.

We're not scared.
We're just afraid.

Not a Male

The horse that was captured on film
wasn't a him
we don't think.
The shot was of his face,
a really tight close up.
We chose it from a bin
of loose pictures for sale.
He wasn't a male
we don't think
cause he had a pretty pink collar on.

Cookout My Idea

The Greenway is a good spot
to girl out down by the river.
The public girls you fill with charcoal,
and the flames in the dusk light.
The agents in the glass cases are dead.
They were orange on the lampposts
when they worked.
Everybody brought a meat,
and the girl is just about ready.
It's the North Oconee.
The Middle is west of here,
and I'll take a break from my steak
to shine the flashlight for a while.

Produce Section

Recorded thunder and strobes.
The mist is silvery
where the aisles open to the back corner.
Floating down
to the waxed red and green
sex appeals
against the wall under a slanted mirror.

We Eat Cheap

We eat cheap
when we don't eat for a week.

I tripped because of hunger
and rolled under a public bush,
but I spit a dead leaf out.

Met the Garrisons for dinner.
The rolls were fantastic,
and the water had ice.
Explained we were saving
for a trip to Crooklyn.

At home, we locked ourselves
in the mud closet.
It had ducts and vents but no windows.

Looking out at the lush backyard—
its fluorescent day glow—
had made us feel too hungry to save.

Went Well

Sup sup
in the hot condo
and grade a dish
by her swelter tank.
The co-worker's mind and black bangs
are on it,
and the casual smoke rise
was once liquid in the pan.

No Cute

A soap bubble formed
over the top of the filter basket
when I washed our coffee equipment.

The horizontal greeting card sat in the setting sun
all week like a paper pup tent,
giving its print away by fading,
so it's almost blank now.

I washed some glasses next.

Things crawl up out of the sink at night,
and who knows what you have on your hands
when you dig for ice.

I Found the Universal Remote

The sun a gold foil
above the construction paper gulf.
A green stripe of nail polish
for the first sandbar.
Cardboard people are tan.
A broken down box is land.
Dyed Stayfree for the pool.
Crewelwork swatch for the yard.
We worked hard on this
for twenty minutes
during *The Cosby Show*.

Burgundy Bruise

Your mouth does funny work
on the bruise on my hand
like the damage you've seen at the fruit stand
in Newport News.
This is my strangest bruise
under your funny mouth.

Lampless in Daylight

Got sick
and nobody understood
because I looked good.
I lost ten pounds.

She was aggressive at me
then penultimate in the worst way.
I was the end,
and she lay there
next to me.

Heating Pad

The flannel cover on our heating pad
represents the McIntosh klan.
Planning to sand your eyes,
is the mayor of the metropolis
whose jet flies leading
a hot contrail
the color of soup in the navy sky out there.

If you can't get to sleep,
think how your body is dark inside,
so we can't watch the pills shrink
and drift to heal your hip.

From the electric nest of heating pad,
the beam of magic sends.
Make her the cutest that I've ever seen.

Pinched Nerve

The phone behind the counter,
behind the glass,
over in the corner next to
the jungle-sized poinsettia.
Her gelled blond hair
stuck to a red leaf
and confused her, so
yes ma'am, Andrew.

The effleurage went well
in the dark.
She didn't think
she liked effleurage.
I changed her mind cause
I'm good at effleurage,
and the little hairs,
they're blond.
What a pleasing trichoesthesia,
and my fingers
like the bug legs
of water walkers,
walking like skating.

Screaming pain in the night
is blue and red.
Night vision coming on.
Hobble to the cushion
where the universal remote is pushing
down to the crumbs and coins.
The sun will make everything better.
Will will it up myself.
Will rise it with my mind.

God sees with the sun,
so he's sightless at night.
So lonely outside his lids.
I will feel good again
and picture having fun
while lots of cash is won
on the late-night game show.

The gold ring matched
the gold eyeglass frames,
matched the tie tack,
matched the magazine rack.
This is he.
He is this
in the middle of himself
on the corner for years.
We've known him behind the trees.
We've known his glass front.
He is day bright fluorescent,
and a precise squint at the counter.
I smell the cold saline,
pepper and *l'eau*.
The first plastic ever made
hangs on the planks
behind the neon curves,
burning quiet except for a hum,
a human um.
Opening his mouth and closing it,
and the white hair matched
the white capsules,
matched the bottle cap,
matched the wax bag.
I'm up to my ears here.
I'll get back to you later on that.

You're a great boyfriend or whatever.
You're a great husband.

Part VI

*The toro breaks, and the toro bust must be a C, was a B
back during virginity, back there at the fair when the clubs were
judges and husbandry was on the mind, wearing a darling gold
leash. But there is cotton candy in the teeth, in the muzzle causing
drool strings.*

I Love Your Sister Too

When people like what they like,
they hear and know a time.
On your screen porch
listening to the stereo
tuned to a station playing
composition *Misterioso*.
Your sister has on,
she just is wearing,
turning over saying turn it up.

Her skin and a patterned tent,
a bent knee drives the toe.
Cool of the potted plants,
distress of the planted plants,
and it's not right
how the dirt is clammy
and the mouth of the daffodil
won't shut up.

When I was a baby,
I lay awake.
I lay still,
but they came
and checked on me anyway.

The boards of the porch,
sun scorched.
It's stuck in the grass
and yellow screaming.
Your sister in the yard
without your parents.
I'm elbows on the frontier table.

You never know
how calm you can be
when trumpets play crazy
with each other,
and the bark crackles
with claws running over it.

Light reflects the hardwood white,
and the grotto of a throat rests
behind the speaker mesh
between the songs.
Another one is on
all day,
and the skin and breeze
don't leave.

The bottle bounces
in the tall grass by the road.
Dad, your sister said,
you don't seem
like the type to litter.
Dropping artifacts all the time.

I heard it shaking branches.
I heard it decorating limbs
with the trash that's been gray forever.
Clever aggregate
sat up and laid back down.
The poster of a clown
hangs on the back of her door.

You call your dad Greg
as a joke.
Your sister calls him slow poke
on the way to the car.
See how far away
the keyless entry works.
Pretty orange blink for noon.

The painted clown face scares me away.

The painted clown face, behind it dressing.
Stall in the hall. I don't like her.
No, not like that.
She sounds like baby's breath
through a distant monitor.

Let's all sit down and eat together.
There's not enough room.
Yes there is.
I'll sit on the floor.
Sit Indian-style.
Let's all come around together.
What are we having?
I'll ask the blessing.
Like the fist of rock,
all unusual colored
from the trip to the creek house
is a door stop.
Amanda says Greg made
the marching band cool again.
It was your sister though,
moistening her reed.

A paragraph describing her torso
printed in white ink
started in the slow blue sky
and ended overlaying the roof of the garage
just like a page from a catalogue.

Your sister,
I missed her the whole time she was gone
to answer the phone.
It was for your mother.
I love her
for having you two.
We were in the living room
with the TV going,
blue in the room
and against the walls
when I hoped against the florist.

He's not a florist?
He just showed up
for a date with your sister?

Hush daffodil.
Your neighbors call.
Our bed is too noisy.
All the chorus growing in it
won't scream lower today.
I'll tell them in the shadows
by the computer desk.
Imagine the whole yard
full of your sister sunning
and sitting up from her dress.
Leaning on the paper mess
in the dark under the stairs.
Tiny and pink,
I think the top is see-through.
The back door is open.
I wouldn't say way open.

When nipples were invented
we heard a gong in the dawn.
The birth was only a day long,
and she was born with parts like you
and parts like your mother too.
Mothers feed sisters food,
and sisters share nightgowns
when the cicadas make sounds,
and the beginning of time
wakes them through the blinds
when their eyes crown in their lids
like the tops of their heads did.
You love your sister.
Your sister loves you, and you love me.
Nodding yes is the confession,
and your parts let me know
you two are kin.
Let me in. Let me in. Let me in,
and tell me your sister secrets.

Like did she whisper in your ear
lush stuff about handsome muscles
and running through the woods
to a mixture of thighs,
like raw dough on the dead leaf bed?
That's not what I said,
and I didn't mean it like that.
Look, I like your look-alike.
I meant the distribution of dreams
across the whole world.
Tiny and pink,
underneath the sheets.
Tiny and pink,
gently pulled by teeth.

When I was a baby,
I lay awake.
I lay still
and watched the headlights fill
the wall beside my head.
Instead of supper,
put us to bed on the upper floor.
Eyes in the dark
shine like buried bulbs,
and your sister is a different version
of a song I've heard before.
It comes on
through the stereo foam,
and I accidentally stand up naked.

The hook of the screen
shakes, swings.

Nightshirt

Got a pink and white
Ginobili jersey
that comes down long,
from torso to knee
in pink.
I cut the tags off
even though
the neck is low.
They're normally black and white too.

Part VII

The host started it. He asked us to play and even went in through the French doors to get his guitar. "I don't think we can do a song tonight," I said.

"I get too nervous, like even thinking about it now, my heart is beating hard. I can feel it against my shirt," she said.

The string of white lights came up out of the plug in the brick side of their house, and they had wrapped the strand in the wooden structure of the canvas patio umbrella. The faces sitting underneath were lit up looking at us.

"Plus we would need our laptop to give you the full effect," I said.

"Or labtop as the guy on the infomercial calls it," she said.

"We can make the beat for you," said the hostess, and everyone tried his knuckles and fists on the glass tabletop to see how it would sound. The silverware rattled, and the white light reflections in the knife blades rocked.

Spinning Sea Glass

Got up from the table
and went to the marina,
read Cataleena
and the other names of boats.
Flirt, Roxanne and Sea Oats,
but my favorite is Cataleena
sitting still now in the marina.
I'm a friend of the family now,
painting cursive on the bow,
Cataleena in black.

I am with some wild ones here,
them who fed me beer
and took me on Cataleena,
way out to a haunting blue.
I knew the sea was deeper than the sky,
and I was suspended between them both,
host to none and guest of neither,
and born from mostly dealing through boards,
our concept of the sea was only half-formed.

I was told by my father-in-law
in the pool behind the waterfall.

I sat above the wide sea today
and imagined you loving the crew
below deck with your suit damp still.
Watch me pop my dramamine pill
and slide the sliding glass
and spin the spinning sea glass.
The sandy shadows keep flat
under all the tinted lenses stacked as sea,

and Cataleena, raised on the concave,
expects the convex next
with me in her open-fisted grip,
recalling the recommendations of my form
on this fiberglass imitation of my habitat.
That's what I've heard a boat is.

I was told by my father-in-law
in the pool behind the waterfall.

I dunk a bucket into the sea
and put it on Cateleena's bow.
The water inside is not the sea,
and standing beside it, I am not me.
How dissociative is the fugue from elements.

We will make the land seem strange,
and a palm tree will look deranged,
shaking fronds like a sycophant
in the condo courtyard
and the little gravel paths.

A panting lizard has passed
wheezing now on a leathery leaf.
My belief in these creatures is gone,
and home is a theory I've rejected with the dust.
My job is to tug on snappers
where the fattest ones nap
without blinking in the deep.
One too short to keep,
we tattooed his bright scales.
They were red. We made them purple.
They were red. We made them green.
They were red. We made them olive,
and I looked at the coral sclera,
a ring around the pupil,
metallic like tinfoil mascara.
Animals have the prettiest makeup and hair.

But now is now, calmly seizing

and now can be forever or a season.
Now is in me with a force I can feel.
We started dating,
and I felt it. Felt that I knew now,
and it was lifted up in front of me
like the prismatic belly of an airborne dolphin,
and my before was what a ghost had done.

Run run run your boat.
Run her out to sea.

Now is now and now is enough,
and Cataleena is in the gulf.
Hit by the mist, I'm happy.
Serene in the marina, I'm resting.
Drinking an orange dusk toddy
and throwing husks and crusts to a lazy noddy.
The food was shucked on the table,
and the oyster juice,
mixed with the mist of a lemon,
has gone inside my wrists
behind a line of sun all day.
The glow of juices trades to you somehow,
and I see the transfer through your palm in the dark house,
our bodies in the covers
glowing like phosphorescence dredged by a ship.

Lapis lazuli,
I thought you knew me.
Take me down to the waves,
my prince.

We are not awake, but we somehow laugh.
We are not the waves, but we want to be.

Centerpiece

Pregnant please
he's not capable.
Seed please
grow a woman or a man.
Grrr grr grreenery is shrubbery,
rubs me past
I pass down the garden path.
Breast as buds
they'll open in the morning.
The boring body hair
makes shadows on the skin.
Pregnant please
he's not kin
to the lineage,
the lineage of men.
Pretend he is botanical
and lock pure essence
in the pleasant seed.
Feed the baby
by sucking it on a twig.
The birthmark is trained
to look like a navel.
I open you to know you
and blow you to grow you,
falling down paths
and muddy bottom dweller.
She grew up in the cellar of a womb
and bloomed in the bull days.
The cockamamie mammie
put her on the rug
too far away to hug
the floral thorns

of the centerpiece
the centerpiece
the ce ce ce ce centerpiece.

Vicious

You were kind of vicious
in the clothes you wore to sleep,
a dress with silver stitches,
no pants because of the heat.

In last week's nap,
some change fell out of my pants.
Metal money in our sheets,
and a dime stuck to your thigh.

You were kind of vicious
when we went to Tennessee.
The eels and flashing fishes
were prisoners you wanted to free.

In scanning bands of light
that the water shapes and sends,
you kissed your own arm again
on the inside where it bends.

You were kind of vicious.

Part VIII

The conversation about fishing took place on the patio in the morning. Everyone ate breakfast together at metal tables, and the girls wore their sunglasses against the low sun glancing off the water. I couldn't see their eyes.

He took up talking again right where he had left off the night before. "Man, I love king. They're my favorite. King are beautiful, and they fight like hell. We used to have grills out at the end of the pier, and we were gutting them and having supper right out of the water, you know, basically," he said.

She took a bite of her omelet and then tried to lean against the cool metal back of her chair. She made a noise that I liked and sat up straight again. Still in the backless dress she had worn to the party, the sequins were catching the sun like silver fish scales.

Late Party Feeling

The midnight rode a zebra in,
and it told everyone I was in love
with the night.
I put my black pocketbook
on the pier mirror
and tried to know my face in the reflection.
Putting on my midnight coat and stockings
was more demure than before.
This tantamount and long stretch of dark
has equal potential at every point.
What wild would we get,
a sonnet read aloud by the crowd
in unison?
And propped foot prophecies about sunglass brunch?
Invite love in on a tiger, someone,
and someone mention I Am.
The greatest word is a mote in the hall.
I can feel its presence behind my buttons,
and the gongs of present time feel like anticipation
back behind my ornaments and nipples.
Hollow worlds are hugging
and meeting in the high ceilings.
They stack like the meals of tomorrow
all covered in gluey brown,
and the paisley shaking in the warm air
might knock us up.
If the apocalypse doesn't come right this minute,
I'll scream.
The fantastic is romantic, and I'm in love tonight
with all there is in heaven and on earth.

Pat

Pat on the lamb,
and knock mud from its wool skirt,
just like the one you wear to Brenau
in the cafeteria with powdered brow
and a South African midknight halved on your breakfast tray.
Tuesday can't go by yesterday today,
and you've been gone a little while now.
Take it tight to its shepherd
who lives in the butler building on the hill.
See the four-wheeler still and silhouetted.
A lamb that's petted is a lamb that runs.
Dote on the pat,
but before the storm,
drive her back to the limestone hall and her dorm.
She has her knees to hug
and decorous mud to knock from her skirt.

Decoration Everywhere

Having the dragonfly on my shoulder
touched up.
The buzzing is cold,
and the ink smell is tremendous.
I hear his wings,
and I rub my hand by
the plants I pass in the garden.
Sweet little brick walk
meanders so.
He grips me by the arm
with his latex glove on.
A couple of different options in the courtyard
where we can eat
sitting at wire tables and chairs.
I can see in the mirror he gives me.
The colors are popping again.

Dolfina Glib

All the girls I've known
live in the wall behind my bed,
and they watch my wife
lie on the aqua sheets
stiff and hot after the laundromat.
She wipes away the hair stuck to her cheek,
and they come helping out of the wall for me
to decorate her with dropped lala lilies
and califloral petalapolies.
The rouge they smear across her belly
is the seedless meat of a watermelly,
and her topiary is too Brazilian to absorb,
the deliscence of the glittered perfume in the room,
floating down through the sunlight
like a handful of shell dust sinking through the gulf blue,
and the airbrush used on her lips
was heavy and royalty flavored.
It's been a taciturnity since she spoke dolfina glib,
but the recourse did her good.
My travel mug and dishes chattered with her in the sink tonight,
and her shutter was muscular against my own.

Marble

The horrible marble across my knuckles
smells like land.
I don't want the marble on my hand.
I want you to hold the marble
where you keep it in your shade.
I'm not ready to be made
and live with fancy rocks.
If you call me Crystal,
I have to hang from chandeliers,
and if I'm not handsome,
I'm bagged as gravel,
cheap as quartz in the store room.
You're wiping marble from my stomach.

Illiterati

I wish I could read
and know what every word means.
The birthplace of modern thinking
is sinking into the canals.
The boat is stretched out long in the afternoon stars.
I read until midnight by lamp.
I read about the Huxtables
taking a long vacation.
All the words were harmonious I know,
but the meanings shot by me in volleys.
I read to the constable
riding on his beat in the bow.
At one word I didn't know,
(in the acres of ancient paragraphs)
he paused
content to drift on sticking done.

Foreign Party

The party's back there
where all the legs hang off the seawall
and lift when the mists are exploding.
The voices sound like party voices,
and my own a ghost's
when I talk to myself.

Say I'm stuck on the beach slope
to the east a mountain
to the west a fountain
with people crowded around in the square.
A sky with stars seems messy and cold,
and under the ocean is hellish and old.
Sharks of prehistory are whipping tails
with giant muscles in the water.

A dark fountain or a black fountain
holding the rim, holding him
before the patio of night glow.

They're handsome in Italian clothes
that shine in the festival lights,
round on the wire and
screwed in so feminine,
and how can the salt bombs rise so large
out of flatness and glass
lying so flush with the purple sky?
I've seen beauty die
and come to life again,
sitting by the fountain or standing up.

A dark mountain or a black mountain

holding a tree, holding an animal
with glowing eyes and a medicinal grip.

Look out or excuse me,
a seawall baking in the thigh heat.
A section of dress flutters on the precipice.
Nasty can be either nasty or sexy.
It depends on the seawall
and where the ice cube falls
that slides off your lip when you try
to bite it into water.

The fishing conversation went well
on the patio in the morning.

Luggage as Seat

The luggage was big
on the carpet lobby
and lobby smelling
arm chair with emptiness,
looks good without me in it.
So luggage as seat,
mug handles,
love handles,
waiting for a transfer.

Part IX

He walked away from the party. The water and the sky were different colors of darkness. The rental catamarans had been pulled way up through the white sand so there was no way high tide could come and drag them out to sea. He lay down on the stretched canvas anyway and looked up at the sky. He sang, "I love you, Jesus Christ. Jesus Christ, I love you. Yes, I do." Water welled from his eyes. The stars were blurred for him then, but the voices coming from the party were still very clear.

Ethereal for Real

Ethereal for real
like taking something
out of the wind,
holding it for a while,
then putting it in my hooded sweatshirt.
The shotgun pocket,
I sleeve stuff from both ends
until I can get it to the park across from my house.
That's where I take it out again
all over the trees and branches,
getting it all over everything.
Oh, ethereal when I let it out.

Blew on a Tree

Blew on the end of a tree.
It was part of a tree that was in my face,
holding leaves out of burgundy shoots.
Tried to make it look like the wind was blowing it.

It shook,
but not like when the wind does it.

The wind does it better.
I tried my best.

Every Child Is Poor

Mad at mom
a lot in the parking lot.
The picture frames cost the same
as the toucans for sale.
When I saw the receipt,
I knew I could have petted their beaks.
They were in a cage to be sold.
I wanted the toucans.
The wind blew into my hands,
and it felt like there was something there to hold.

Part X

The bull saw an entire November in 1986 that had trouble in it. The calendar was messy with red marker, and the bull still has a pair of jeans that accidentally took in some ink.

Sapin Cisco

Mommy does not love me
or my skateboard that say thrash.
I rode it down the hall,
so I put our picture in the trash.
Rode it on my belly
and crast the mirro down.
We stood in front of a picture of the woods,
but we were in a town
when I was a baby enough to hold.
Rolled today into the mirro,
and now I have to go to Sapin Cisco
where a runaway go to a lot.

Dirt Bike Trip

Delivered a knapsack full of flower petals
and some blooms and leaf trash.
I pulled out the stash
at the feet of a yesteryear gypsy.
Stand of trees with natural seats.
It was a cross-country dirt bike trip,
a forbidden idea,
and I parked it with the engine whining high.
Kickstand in the canopy,
all she could stand of me,
I gave her in an instant.
And my front tire rose to a ghostly wheelie
when I motocrossed the shade line.

Kid Clamorous

My new shoes almost fit
in the diamonds
of the chain-linked fence I'm climbing.
They were shining
and reflecting, so I might get caught.
I don't care for that
or the appletini
my friend had me drink
before we were about to write.
But suffering gets more fun
the older you get.
Little me couldn't even be yelled at.
He'd leave home or pretend to.
When I get to age thirty-three—
watch out—
I'm going to love to suffer,
throwing up symbols
that will sock you
and finding work in nothing.

Whispering Red

Things work out in a rented room
like pulling on the drawer
under the remote bolted down
and a tabletop for whatever
I got to spread out,
maps and brochures.
Here's a receipt I wrote on.

A man can't need anything
or ever check himself in the mirror,
but my Braves hat is too new looking.
I didn't want to find a broken in one
cause I don't like other people's dirt.
They told her, and she told me.

Rumor Will Float

Rumor will float
for a while
then hang on the roots
and the litter foam.

The truth will sink
after a deep bomb
chokes the surface of the water,
and it will sit up tall on the bottom
like the child who knew I lied.

Kid of the Country

My mouth is full of fog.
I leave it open a lot,
and my braces are like
the Golden Gate Bridge
spanning the mouth of the bay
when I smile prehistorical
and slow like the beginning of time
when the Americas broke off
and barreled over here
rolling on a pile of core fire
that left mantle cinders
and dust of phlogiston
blinking in the sea.
Always lapping at the heels of land,
what about me breaks like foam?
I can taste the ancients
that were left behind
when I lick a finger dipped in the cold.
The salt is sweat from the maniacs of old,
clicking sticks by the cooking pit,
ribcages the borderland
between shadow and glow.

But the man in the swimming cap
is swimming by slow,
and I have to get back
to the Pacific Heights Inn.
The Friday night rollerbladers
skate right by the place.
I wrote on one's face
a bright one you can read.

Nightspot Spell

Got a spell idea to put on myself.
Took a red stocking cap off the shelf,
unfolded its warming ways
and put it on backwards
on the way to a nightspot.
Hot mob showing torso sweat.
Bet nobody will even notice my hat.
The dance lights mottled the dance floor,
and I used a burgundy bottle
to creek heat down my cheeks.
I cried into my mouth
until I was cured by a hat snatcher
who joker jumped through the crowd,
and my spell was finally off me then.
Spirits in the rafters bumped their heads,
said what.

Part XI

There once was a toro that had sin in it, and it wandered into the construction site. Cut sections of yellow rope lay knotted together in a puddle. The toro looked at it with a dirty mind and saw a dead starfish in a tide pool. In the thought cloud between its horns, you can read all the symbols that stand for cussing.

Straightening Up

I like the book on top of the newspaper.
I like the cell phone on top of the newspaper
next to the book.
I like the newspaper on the table next to my chair
where I might read.
Looks like I could if I wanted to,
a newspaper, a book, a text.

Lily Olive and K. Poncé

The jewelry in the sheets
are gold chains in the linens.
She can arrange them there, or
she can do whatever she wants
in her own apartment,
listen to the telephone ring
but ignore the radio,
stretch out on the bed
and have a bad dream.

Gold soft focus light,
burnt yellow apartment furniture
in the background.
It must be early light in the window.
The magazine on the sink
she reads with her hands in her hair.

I need someone to flip the pages.
New York outside is moving.
New York is great.
I had lots of friends in Florida.
I miss Florida.
The guy friends walked like men
in the bars after hauling snapper in,
and the wire chairs on the patio,
we sat there all the time.

Turbulence in the jet,
and I banged my elbow
on the bathroom sink.
In the last row,
fell in a seat next to him,

Kim from Europe.
Took a cigarette
from his silver box.
K. Poncé engraved.
No one waiting at the gate to explain to,
I was nervous.
I thought it would relax me.
The jet was jumping in the sky.

It was a nine page document.
I three-hole punched it,
made a tab for it
and before I filed it in the binder,
I stuck it in the typewriter
and snapped my initials and the date
in the corner on the bottom right.
The mai tais will taste alright tonight,
and if he offers me a cigarette three times,
I promise to refuse it twice
and smoke in the colored lights of the dance floor.

How can I flirt
if she doesn't show up to work?
How can I like a dial tone
if she never answers the phone?
I broke into Lily's apartment.
The bathroom had perfume
in the shower steam.
She had just gotten dressed and left.
I noticed everything,
right down to the teardrops,
gray on a white magazine page.
Making snakes out of gold chains on the sheets,
 I wrinkled my gray suit
and sat and saw the street
the way she sees it.
There are duplicate bumper stickers
on the car always parked across the street.

White meat of a green apple

dipped in the fondue.
A tea candle can really keep it melted.
It's enough heat.
The name of the flute music.
I held a skewer while sitting cross-legged on a pillow,
and the row of beads divided the two rooms.
The flute came through.
I saw a pair of lips in the straw hair,
and they touched the metal tube.
The beads were out of focus
when we were clear.
It's enough heat.

I doodled blue vines on a pad
then put the cap between my lips
to think about an offshoot.
The air has to be way down
and the canopy so shady
to make us feel like coffee
on such a hot morning.
The sun glowing the water
to translucent blue
and see-through green.
See a bather topless in the big waves.
Her skin is like my shade-grown here.
Then Kim again, once more then never again,
his dark hair long now like what I've drawn,
blowing through his steam and walking.

My Cousin's for Christmas

My cousin's for Christmas,
a big Florida yard.
Do you eat crawfish?
I don't know what that is.
Like crawfish?
I don't know what that is,
so I can't say
whether I eat it or not.

Sit Song

There's more time
to think down here.
Everything's based on nature,
and she's a slow birth mother
to my voice,
winding out from deep
in my head and sounding
like a defunct cassette at first,
then revving to singing
like History the Giant in a choir voice,
backed by the beating of the earth
and feathered buddies whistling
whatever they feel like.
Someone's lost in the shallow canyon.

Time for Time

You are drinking expensive coffee.
You are thinking about a promotion.
Intimate with a few melodies
with lyrics about outside.
All the windows and doors are open,
and there are no lights on,
lampless in daylight.

The cords stretched across the rug
are deciding what to do about work.
You want to get things on your pants,
and you want those pants to be jeans.

The roof needs repair.
You see that.

I recorded the road noise.
Nobody came,
so I didn't record anything.

Invited a Mirage In

Took a picture of a mirage,
but it didn't develop,
just the Florida road
glossy and bright
and all the stuff up ahead.

The neon nighttime
pulled a very dirty trick.
I saw an alibi in the flowerbed
and sat there until
that girl got bark on her bikini too,
but you didn't develop,
just my exaggerated
shadow on the motel wall,
and I paid for the shade,
just because they charged me for it.

Spending Time

Sending all our bought air out,
you know how to keep a door closed.
I grow sometimes too
when on the balcony,
I answer flippant on a flip phone.

She's calling crunching ice though.
That's alright. I picture it,
her mouth melting it.
The expensive minutes I buy,
condition my time
like a real dear temperature in the room.

Construction Job

In my reflective vest and hard hat,
I stood embarrassed
watching Jorge bang the street
with the cupped metal paw
of a backhoe.
It sounded off the buildings
and rang through their pale shadows.
He in a hurry looked on, walking to his office
with a sleeve on his paper coffee cup
and cuffs white-blue in the suit shadows.

I worked in an office too once.

Jorge in the glass cabin,
on display like an art exhibit.

My Mountain Dew,
the cap twisted over an hour ago,
sat flat and glowing.
I looked at it sick,
like the Degas girl at her absinthe glass,
the rest of the table humming.

Jorge was performing.
He was trying to open her up,
and the pipes, once seen,
felt tender to be exposed,
I know.

Scrape Together

You correct me
when my polo buttons at my nape
and ask me where I'm living
and say my name,
but I have grits.
They're steaming in styrene.

Don't say my name
like the bells on the door
say I'm here.
Say in the back.
Stay nothing.
You know I eat them outside
where nobody sees my habits.

I have manners like salt in warm water.

Like This

Been wandering around the yard
without a shirt.
Haven't cut my hair
since one summer,
but it's not any longer.
It's more like yards of copper wire,
off the spool and curling in the mud.
You should see it sometime
by photo or in person.

I point my head downhill
when I lie on a slope.
Blood in the head makes
the shadowed cloud bottoms pop against
the hot white sides and tops.
Now I know some things I really believe in,
like rest assured
and God
and everything you did should be cured,
my baby, my baby, my pal.

Impersonations

I can talk like you,
and you can talk like your friend.
Wide tongue on the ridged roof of your mouth.
The clear gulf rolling makes the same pattern in the sand.
Walking on it makes my arches hurt.
They're telling me through my nerves,
and they can talk like seagulls.

Mile is a Walk

Walking with salt
between my thighs,
a mile is a walk to the pier.
Hear stilts in a crashing white,
open air story of height.
You're somewhere with clothes
all over you maybe,
but even in winter, everybody saw
the small of your back when you bent over.
Peek of pink lace over a lip of denim,
I saw you not in them.
Love is a walk to the pier.
Here with a burning in my suit
and a turning around to do.

Part XII

Black horns in white sand. White grandstand with black people. White church steeple in the black sky reminds us of when the bull walked by. Black hoofs clicking on white tile. White profile on black canvas, and this modern streak of green is supposed to represent certain things. But I don't know whether I like it or not. I honesty do not know.

Went to the Garden Alone

Woke a homeless up in the garden at dawn.
He said from an azalea,
the sun's about to come up.
When it does, I'm going to blow it out.
I can blow it out like a candle.
Take a deep breath and help me.

Dawn Exercise

Killed another week
with my feet on the concrete.
Every moon-soaked morning,
running like my forefathers
on the reckoning of time.
Put ground back there
and long to lockstep
with a pack of early men.
Since I have it and no one is here,
move me to travel me
like the ancient pitter-patter
in the boiling plains dawn.
I must love running shoes
with bright colors and double-knots.
The rising of the east heat
comes with working
and mixes weird with the streetlights,
so I know I could go forever
back to the first yawn of man.
But there is pajamaed Ostara,
the passionate host of tradition's beginnings
with gold crescent rolls
in the lamplight of the condo.
Oh yeah,
I did.
I did break a sweat,
undoing my drawstrings
and taking down my hood.

Medieval

You are not a transcendentalist,
but you are organic like
the sound a harpsichord makes
in old Britain before a king.
And transparent,
but not like a walking eyeball,
like an hourglass, shapely trinket,
truncata blue anima mundi,
and your voice sounds like
sand hitting a towel.
A whispered philosophy
resonates like the bang of a monk's gong.
Joseph A. Wilfong
has a wrought-iron gate dedicated to his memory.
I remember your face from a few seconds ago
in the sunken courtyard beside the church,
and the people on the street see me
smiling weird to myself.

Springtime Outside the Restaurant

Everyone is hot
because of the dragon
silkscreened on your dark blue shirt.
He's not breathing.
He didn't mean it.
Tail all tucked like
the butt of a brass instrument.
He didn't say anything like Clint,
"I'm moving to Hawaii to work on a golf course."
Your shirt is the perfect mixture
of humility and aggression.
They all hum aggression
without thinking in the street
and show up with smoke
in the corners where their lips meet.
But shirts, never people
are tossable when they stop to fit,
even when they're talking chit,
mad and cheap, so that it
loops in your head when you try to sleep.

It's springtime outside the restaurant.
Every taillight is red.

Black Man in a Black Light

In love with a homeless.
Where will you seat him anyway
say I invite him up?
The black velvet sofa
with neon plant print?
And glowing beads?
A black man in a black light
is hard to imagine,
but fashion is chest hair showing,
and it will still be growing
when heaven's alleys are home.

Gift of Shades

I left work before time,
and drove so a black
sleep came up
like a heavy well of lava.
I pulled over and still faced
the electric sun
burning like a fake streetlight
and doing a dramatic impression of
my worn out face.
I found a wrapped box in the console.
It was a gift pair of Ray Ban's from you.
Sleeping wearing them is
the slick ribbon in my lap.

Sciatica Song

When are you going to steal my mind
and use my star?
When I get to the gates of heaven,
someone will show me the way to you.
I'm sorry, but in my imagination,
you die before I do.
You will be in the light of rainbow colors.
You will no more be in skin colors.
You'll never again have a spectrum to hold you back.

Torsino

Most of the body
got the idea to it
from nothing.
Checking on bare.
Bending backwards.
Structure in the afternoon.
Body lots of time
and parts against,
divided and working.
Sexes and watching water boil.
The light of some
on your body,
the main part is for it.

Aesthete Above All

Love is every color,
red in a conflagration of enemies
and floral wet gear near untanned skin,
lenses so dark I have to touch my nose
to yours to look into your eyes,
pink in the things we cut from paper
and wear in our hair,
like the butterscotch wrapper
that rose from the console
when we rolled down the windows,
tinted purple, the color of street love.
An aesthete above all,
and to think I thought with my pecker once.

Rainbow at Night

The rainbow was in Georgia
for a while.
Then it moved east behind drapes of rain.

The rainbow was in Abbeville, South Carolina
while my cousin had her foot propped in the afternoon.
Then it moved east behind drapes of rain.

The rainbow was over the ocean
throughout the night.
All the fish looked up.

Tiberian Breakfast

So should the ocean get glassy.
In cold and careful morning, I wake up
when my arm comes out of my sleeping bag,
and I blink in the green glowing dome of our canvas tent.

The performance vest is snapped across my chest,
and my ribs are kind of warm.
I have a book in my pocket,
but all we read are matches flaps,
and all we drink are Pabsts
while I crave some charming hint of substance,
leaking eyes or a twitching upper lip,
a ziploc of coffee or a magazine filled with interviews.

I had things to think
and didn't want to wake you.
Mare Bear, I'd wade with you
for broken shells with holes like hasps
and pancreatic sea glass
and driftwood.
I love you with all my liver, *mon petit chou,*
and I would wade my tarsals away.
I would comb my ankles gone
and hold all of your wet things in my pocket
for a little more time.

This will be the great breakfast verse,
me on the beach heating flanks of perch.
The fire, the only thing not brown or drab,
sits on the driftwood hissing with dew,
and this yellow light is yelling loud.
This firelight is compelling the crowd.
I see them now, staring not-so-brightly on the bow,

and their boat foam and motor foam is waking the drowned,
breaking our dearest ocean's concentration.

The incident of the black seagull,
remember its head looked pretty smart,
and there was an art to its bread begging.
Bread of chest and wine of bloodline,
it bathed the crumbs from its beak in the tide.
The little sin-eater tried to light on my lap
while I sat in the folding chair studying the map.
You came half an inch from Magdala, Magpie,
oh which was well, the western coast.
We'll come back some other spring, I hope,
when all is purple and heliotrope.
But my beard is weird now with crusts of salt,
and the disciples notice me. They are not far off.

Darrell Kinsey, Jr.
Athens, Georgia

www.ingramcontent.com/pod-product-compliance
Lightning Source LLC
LaVergne TN
LVHW011234080426
835509LV00005B/498